LIFE PICTURE PUZZLE

WELCOME TO LIFE'S ELEVENTH
PICTURE
PUZZLE
BOOK

We've been across America and around the world with our Picture Puzzle books. Our spot-the-difference puzzles have celebrated the holidays, gone on vacation, and even gone to the dogs, camels, elephants, giraffes, and polar bears. We've created mystery and whodunit puzzles out of timeless characters, such as Sherlock Holmes and the Thin Man, using photos from classic movies and television series. And it's all been tremendous fun. We've had a wonderful time carefully shaping each puzzle to offer just the right amount of challenge to new puzzlers, while making sure to find a fresh approach for each new book—keeping things lively for our most loyal puzzlers. And we must be doing something right because LIFE's Picture Puzzle books remain the most popular of the genre. Thank you.

This is our eleventh Picture Puzzle book. Hard to believe. With ten under our belt, we looked upon this one as something of a new beginning. As our title indicates, we took it as our mission to focus on the essentials: What is it that makes for the most colorful, most fun, most challenging picture puzzle. What goes into the perfect picture puzzle? We asked our photo editors and our wild-and-crazy Puzzle Master to ask those questions as they approached each page in this book, and we think they've come up with our best collection of puzzles yet. Is the book perfect? Only you can say.

Sticking to the essentials means keeping what works. Our Novice section still offers a gentle introduction for beginning puzzlers. Then we gradually increase the challenge throughout our Master and Expert sections. Think of it as on-the-job training. But a word of warning. By the time you attempt our Genius section, you should be ready to tackle some truly baffling conundrums. Otherwise, we fear these puzzles may master you.

[OUR CUT-UP PUZZLES: EASY AS 1-2-3]

We snipped a photo into four or six pieces. Then we rearranged the pieces and numbered them.

Your mission: Beneath each cut-up puzzle, write the number of the piece in the box where it belongs.

Check the answer key at the back of the book to see what the reassembled image looks like.

[HOW TO PLAY THE PUZZLES]

Staring Contest

Do the tourists ever get the sense that they are being watched?

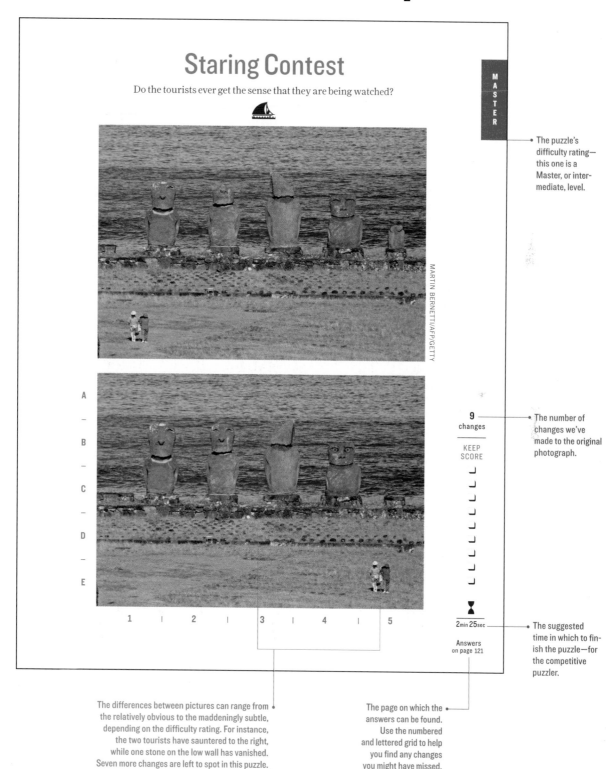

MARTIN BERNETTI/AFP/GETTY

MASTER

The puzzle's difficulty rating—this one is a Master, or intermediate, level.

9 changes

The number of changes we've made to the original photograph.

KEEP SCORE

2min 25sec

The suggested time in which to finish the puzzle—for the competitive puzzler.

Answers on page 121

The differences between pictures can range from the relatively obvious to the maddeningly subtle, depending on the difficulty rating. For instance, the two tourists have sauntered to the right, while one stone on the low wall has vanished. Seven more changes are left to spot in this puzzle.

The page on which the answers can be found. Use the numbered and lettered grid to help you find any changes you might have missed.

LIFE PICTURE PUZZLE

Puzzle Master Michael Roseman
Editor Robert Sullivan
Director of Photography Barbara Baker Burrows
Deputy Picture Editor Christina Lieberman
Copy Editors Marilyn Fu, Parlan McGaw

LIFE Puzzle Books
Managing Editor Bill Shapiro

LIFE Books
President Andrew Blau
Business Manager Roger Adler
Business Development Manager Jeff Burak

Editorial Operations
Richard K. Prue (Director), Brian Fellows (Manager), Keith Aurelio, Charlotte Coco,
Tracey Eure, Kevin Hart, Mert Kerimoglu, Rosalie Khan, Patricia Koh, Marco Lau,
Brian Mai, Po Fung Ng, Rudi Papiri, Robert Pizaro, Barry Pribula, Clara Renauro, Hia Tan,
Vaune Trachtman

Time Home Entertainment
Publisher Richard Fraiman
General Manager Steven Sandonato
Executive Director, Marketing Services Carol Pittard
Director, Retail & Special Sales Tom Mifsud
Director, New Product Development Peter Harper
Director, Bookazine Development & Marketing Laura Adam
Publishing Director, Brand Marketing Joy Butts
Associate General Counsel Helen Wan
Book Production Manager Suzanne Janso
Design & Prepress Manager Anne-Michelle Gallero
Brand Manager Roshni Patel

Special thanks to Christine Austin, Jeremy Biloon, Glenn Buonocore, Jim Childs, Susan
Chodakiewicz, Rose Cirrincione, Jacqueline Fitzgerald, Carrie Frazier, Lauren Hall, Malena
Jones, Brynn Joyce, Mona Li, Robert Marasco, Amy Migliaccio, Kimberly Posa, Brooke
Reger, Dave Rozzelle, Ilene Schreider, Adriana Tierno, Alex Voznesenskiy, Sydney Webber

PUBLISHED BY

LIFE Books

an imprint of Time Home Entertainment Inc.   Vol. 10, No. 9 • October 8, 2010

Copyright © 2010
Time Home Entertainment Inc.
135 West 50th Street
New York, NY 10020

We welcome your comments and suggestions about LIFE Books. Please write to us at:
LIFE Books
Attention: Book Editors
PO Box 11016
Des Moines, IA 50336-1016

If you would like to order any of our hardcover Collector's Edition books, please call us at 1-800-327-6388
(Monday through Friday, 7 a.m. to 8 p.m., or Saturday, 7 a.m. to 6 p.m. Central Time).

READY, SET,
GO!

NOVICE

[
These puzzles are for everyone:
rookies and veterans,
young and old. Start here, and
sharpen your skills.
]

Remember to Floss

My, what big teeth you have!

EITAN ABRAMOVICH/AFP/GETTY

A

—

B

—

C

—

D

—

E

1   2   3   4   5

8
changes

KEEP
SCORE

❏
❏
❏
❏
❏
❏
❏
❏

⧖

2min 10sec

Answers
on page 121

Leap of Faith

The cord won't break. The cord won't break. The cord won't break.

DARRYL LENIUK/GETTY

A
—
B
—
C
—
D
—
E

1   2   3   4   5

7
changes

KEEP
SCORE

☐
☐
☐
☐
☐
☐
☐

⧖
1min 55sec

Answers
on page 121

Land of the Giants . . .

... Or some very tiny horses

A
B
C
D
E

1   2   3   4   5

9
changes

⧖
2min 40sec

Answers
on page 121

KEEP SCORE ★ ❏ ❏ ❏ ❏ ❏ ❏ ❏ ❏ ❏

You've Heard of the Trojan Horse?

Well, don't trust a wooden elephant, either

ROBIN UTRECHT/AFP/GETTY

A — B — C — D — E

1   2   3   4   5

9 changes

⏳ 2min 55sec

Answers on page 121

KEEP SCORE ★ ☐ ☐ ☐ ☐ ☐ ☐ ☐ ☐ ☐

Stairway to Heaven

When it's springtime on China's Great Wall,
everybody feels like getting married

A

B

C

D

E

1   2   3   4   5

7
changes

2min 15sec

Answers
on page 121

KEEP SCORE ★ ❏ ❏ ❏ ❏ ❏ ❏ ❏

Tee Time

And they've got caddies that never talk back

1

2

3

4

5

6

RICHARD ELLIS/GETTY

⧗
0min 30sec

Answer
on page 121

Pass the Hot Sauce

Eats cars for lunch

1

2

3

4

5

GREG WOOD/AFP/GETTY

6

0min 45sec

Answer
on page 121

Crazy, Dude!

The amazing thing is not how well they surf, but that they do surf at all

A

B

C

D

E

1   2   3   4   5

8
changes

KEEP
SCORE

☐
☐
☐
☐
☐
☐
☐
☐

⌛

2min 15sec

Answers
on page 121

Pumping Canine

How many beagle reps can you do?

JUNKO KIMURA/GETTY

A
—
B
—
C
—
D
—
E

1   2   3   4   5

6
changes

2min 10sec

KEEP SCORE ★ ⅃ ⅃ ⅃ ⅃ ⅃ ⅃

Answers
on page 121

Circle of Friends

Off we go into the wild blue yonder

MIKE MYERS/AFP/GETTY

A
—
B
—
C
—
D
—
E

1 | 2 | 3 | 4 | 5

8
changes

2min 50sec

Answers
on page 121

KEEP SCORE ★ ❑ ❑ ❑ ❑ ❑ ❑ ❑ ❑

Head Over Heels

Or is it really heels over head?

7
changes

KEEP
SCORE

☐
☐
☐
☐
☐
☐
☐

⧗

1min 45sec

Answers
on page 122

A

—

B

—

C

—

D

—

E

1 | 2 | 3 | 4 | 5

Bumper-to-Bumper Traffic

Let's hope the brakes are working

MICHAEL JOHN O'NEILL/GETTY

6 changes

KEEP SCORE

2 min 55 sec

Answers on page 122

Symmetry in Stone

The rhythm of life is peaceful at the Taj Mahal

FRANS LEMMENS/GETTY

A

B

C

D

E

1 | 2 | 3 | 4 | 5

8 changes

3min 40sec

Answers on page 122

KEEP SCORE ★ ❏ ❏ ❏ ❏ ❏ ❏ ❏ ❏

Please Don't Feed the Dino

But gentle pats on the head are gratefully accepted

A
—
B
—
C
—
D
—
E

1   2   3   4   5

9
changes

KEEP
SCORE

2min 35sec

Answers
on page 122

Space Age Dubai

Don't let the angle fool you. We're definitely not in Pisa.

MARWAN NAAMANI/AFP/GETTY

10
changes

KEEP
SCORE

❏
❏
❏
❏
❏
❏
❏
❏
❏
❏

⏳

2min 25sec

Answers
on page 122

Flag Day

Something about the photo looks a little staged

NASA

A

B

C

D

E

1   2   3   4   5

8
changes

⏳
2min 45sec

Answers
on page 122

KEEP SCORE ★ ❑ ❑ ❑ ❑ ❑ ❑ ❑ ❑

What's Buggin' You?

The pest control guys have their hands full

A
B
C
D
E

1 2 3 4 5

8
changes

⏳
3min 45sec

Answers
on page 122

KEEP SCORE ★ ❏ ❏ ❏ ❏ ❏ ❏ ❏ ❏

Fishy Business

Separate the water and the air before someone gets eaten

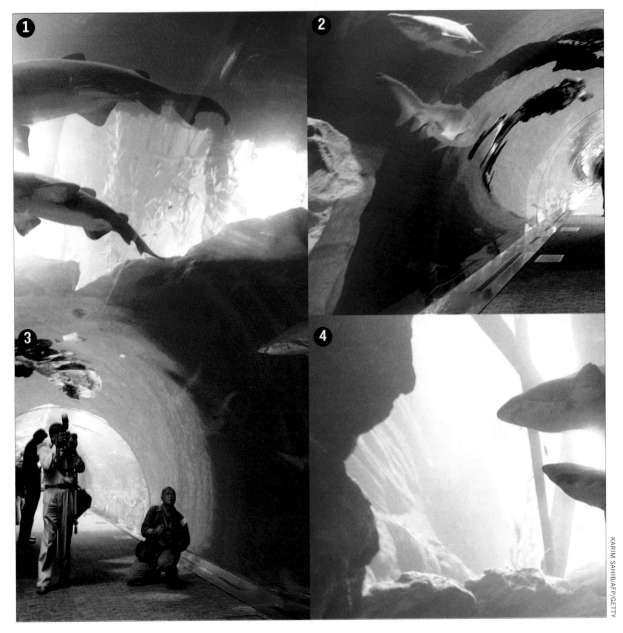

KARIM SAHIB/AFP/GETTY

0min 30sec

Answer
on page 122

KEEP SCORE

Everything's Coming Up Roses

The Tournament of Roses Parade can be great fun, but stay away from the robot's feet

ALBERTO E. RODRIGUEZ/GETTY

KEEP SCORE

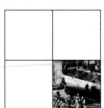

⏳

0min 45sec

Answer
on page 122

Balancing Act

It takes steady nerves to ride the slide

A
—
B
—
C
—
D
—
E

1   2   3   4   5

10
changes

⧖
3min 35sec

Answers
on page 122

KEEP SCORE ★ ❑ ❑ ❑ ❑ ❑ ❑ ❑ ❑ ❑ ❑

Nice Kitties, Nice Kitties

Some catnip would come in handy right about now

EYESWIDEOPEN/GETTY

9
changes

KEEP
SCORE

⏳

3min 55sec

Answers
on page 123

MASTER

[Here, puzzles get
a little harder. You'll
need to raise
your game a level.]

And the Winner Is . . .

… You, by a nose, if you solve this puzzle

FERENC ISZA/AFP/GETTY

10
changes

KEEP
SCORE

⌛
3min 50sec

Answers
on page 123

Cliffhanger

Sometimes you have nowhere to go but up

A

—

B

—

C

—

D

—

E

1 | 2 | 3 | 4 | 5

10
changes
_____

KEEP
SCORE

❑
❑
❑
❑
❑
❑
❑
❑
❑
❑

⧗

3min 15sec

Answers
on page 123

A Walk on the Wild Side

It's no place to space out

STOCKTREK IMAGES/GETTY

5

4

3

2

1

9
changes

KEEP
SCORE

⌣ ⌣ ⌣ ⌣ ⌣ ⌣ ⌣ ⌣ ⌣

⏳

2min 45sec

Answers
on page 123

A

B

C

D

E

Hey There, Little Fella

This looks like the beginning of
a beautiful friendship

A
B
C
D
E

1   2   3   4   5

10
changes

⧗
3min 20sec

Answers
on page 123

KEEP SCORE ★ ❏ ❏ ❏ ❏ ❏ ❏ ❏ ❏ ❏ ❏

Celestial Season

If it's the spring equinox on the Salisbury Plain,
then these must be Druids

A
—
B
—
C
—
D
—
E

1 | 2 | 3 | 4 | 5

11 changes

2min 10sec

Answers
on page 123

KEEP SCORE ★ ❏ ❏ ❏ ❏ ❏ ❏ ❏ ❏ ❏ ❏ ❏

Imperial Waters

This lacks only a czar

A

B

C

12
changes

D

⏳
4min 15sec

Answers
on page 123

E

1 | 2 | 3 | 4 | 5

A Slippery Slope

Getting to the bottom of this puzzle
would be really cool

A

—

B

—

C

—

D

—

E

1   2   3   4   5

9
changes

⧖

3min 10sec

Answers
on page 123

KEEP SCORE ★ ❏ ❏ ❏ ❏ ❏ ❏ ❏ ❏

Poetry in Motion

Unless he belly-flops

PAOLO COCCO/AFP/GETTY

5

4

3

2

1

10
changes

KEEP
SCORE

⧗

2min 45sec

Answers
on page 123

A

B

C

D

E

PICTURE PUZZLE **LIFE** | **57**

Don't Get Snookered

One of these gentlemen isn't quite on cue

1

2

3

4

5

6

0min 45sec

Answer
on page 123

CHINA PHOTOS/GETTY (2)

It's Alive!

Find the altered image and you are a dino-mite puzzler

1

2

3

4

5

6

0min 55sec

Answer
on page 124

Sittin' on Top of the World

Some people will go to great lengths
for a little privacy

PEMBA DORJE SHERPA/AFP/GETTY

A
—
B
—
C
—
D
—
E

1   2   3   4   5

10
changes

3min 15sec

Answers
on page 124

KEEP SCORE ★ ❏ ❏ ❏ ❏ ❏ ❏ ❏ ❏ ❏ ❏

Triangulation

After you solve this puzzle,
you *will* believe in the power of pyramids

SEAN GALLUP/GETTY

A
—
B
—
C
—
D
—
E

1 | 2 | 3 | 4 | 5

9
changes

⧗
3min 35sec

Answers
on page 124

KEEP SCORE ★ ❏ ❏ ❏ ❏ ❏ ❏ ❏ ❏ ❏

On Safari

This long-necked lady asks the universal question "Are we there yet?"

A
B
C
D
E

1 | 2 | 3 | 4 | 5

10
changes

KEEP
SCORE

☐
☐
☐
☐
☐
☐
☐
☐
☐
☐

⏳
3min 35sec

Answers
on page 124

One Hump or Two?

Strange days in Merrie Olde England

A
—
B
—
C
—
D
—
E

1 | 2 | 3 | 4 | 5

9
changes

⧗

3min 35sec

Answers
on page 124

KEEP SCORE ★ ❑ ❑ ❑ ❑ ❑ ❑ ❑ ❑ ❑

Batter Up!

Wonder if he'll slide home

PETER MCBRIDE/AURORA/GETTY

5

4

3

2

1

A | B | C | D | E

10
changes

KEEP
SCORE

❏ ❏ ❏ ❏ ❏ ❏ ❏ ❏ ❏ ❏

3min 55sec

Answers
on page 124

If a Tree Falls . . .

. . . Solutions must be found

A
—
B
—
C
—
D
—
E

1 | 2 | 3 | 4 | 5

9
changes

⌛

2min 50sec

Answers
on page 124

KEEP SCORE ★ ❏ ❏ ❏ ❏ ❏ ❏ ❏ ❏ ❏

The Flowers that Bloom in the Spring

This garden needs order restored

⏳ 1min 35sec

Answer
on page 124

KEEP SCORE

ANDREW HOLT/GETTY

Sky High

In order to solve this, you'll need an aerial perspective

MARC TRIGALOU/GETTY

KEEP SCORE

1min 15sec

Answer
on page 124

Pucker Up

Give 'em a good squeeze and you've got yourself a lot of juice

1

2

3

4

5

6

0min 35sec

Answer
on page 124

EMPORTES JM/GETTY

Big Birds

Which picture is not of a feather?

1

2

3

4

5

6

ZHAO JINGDONG/CHINAFOTO/GETTY

0min 50sec

Answer
on page 124

In the Village

This sleepy coastal hamlet is hiding a lot of secrets

DARRYL LENIUK/GETTY

12
changes

KEEP
SCORE

2min 45sec

Answers
on page 124

EXPERT

[

Only serious puzzlers
dare to tread past this point.
Who's in?

]

Candyland

The taffy has been pulled all out of shape

KEEP SCORE

4min 45sec

Answer
on page 124

Fair Weather Ferry

Is this puzzle a safe harbor for you?

THOMAS MCCONVILLE/PHOTOGRAPHER'S CHOICE/GETTY

12
changes

KEEP
SCORE

⌛
4min 40sec

Answers
on page 125

Like a Neon Cowboy

If you flip the light switch, tourists will come

A

B

C

D

E

1   2   3   4   5

13
changes

KEEP
SCORE

☐
☐
☐
☐
☐
☐
☐
☐
☐
☐
☐
☐
☐

⌛

4min 15sec

Answers
on page 125

A San Francisco Treat

Riding the cable cars is one of this city's famous offerings . . .
as is a certain rice product

A
—
B
—
C
—
D
—
E

1   2   3   4   5

13
changes

⏳
5min 25sec

Answers
on page 125

Pass the Mustard

At low tide, room for a picnic

MERLE SEVERY/NATIONAL GEOGRAPHIC/GETTY

14
changes

KEEP
SCORE

5min 45sec

Answers
on page 125

Pomp and Circumstance

One of these pictures rolls a different way

1

2

3

4

5

6

⏳
1min 35sec

Answer
on page 125

CATE GILLON/GETTY

In the House of the Mouse

It's tea time at Mickey's place

1

2

3

4

5

6

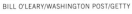
BILL O'LEARY/WASHINGTON POST/GETTY

1min 45sec

Answer
on page 125

Clown Town

Even in New York City,
these folks tend to stand out

A
—
B
—
C
—
D
—
E

1 | 2 | 3 | 4 | 5

14
changes

5min 35sec

Answers
on page 125

KEEP SCORE ★ ❑ ❑ ❑ ❑ ❑ ❑ ❑ ❑ ❑ ❑ ❑ ❑ ❑ ❑

Mirror, Mirror on the Wall

Take a little time to reflect on this one

LOUISA GOULIAMAKI/AFP/GETTY

5

4

3

2

1

13
changes

KEEP
SCORE

❏
❏
❏
❏
❏
❏
❏
❏
❏
❏
❏
❏
❏

⧗
5min 25sec

Answers
on page 125

A | B | C | D | E

GENIUS

[

Finding a single difference
in these puzzles is a
challenge. Finding them all
might be impossible.

]

Hangin' Out
The paintings aren't all that's on display

GRAEME ROBERTSON/GETTY

A
–
B
–
C
–
D
–
E

1   2   3   4   5

14
changes

KEEP
SCORE

⌛
4min 30sec

Answers
on page 126

Changing of the Guard (Again)

We're not at Buckingham Palace anymore, are we?

JOHN BANAGAN/GETTY

16
changes

KEEP
SCORE

❏ ❏ ❏ ❏ ❏ ❏ ❏ ❏ ❏ ❏ ❏ ❏ ❏ ❏ ❏ ❏

5min 25sec

Answers
on page 126

Let Me Out!

The Shuttle begs not to be mothballed

A

B

C

D

E

1   2   3   4   5

JAMES S. M. DONNELL SPACE HANGAR

Fund America's Treasures

15
changes

KEEP
SCORE

❏
❏
❏
❏
❏
❏
❏
❏
❏
❏
❏
❏
❏
❏
❏

⌛
4min 55sec

Answers
on page 126

The Curiosity Shoppe

An Anglophile would have a Dickens of a time choosing what to buy

A
—
B
—
C
—
D
—
E

1   2   3   4   5

16
changes

5min 15sec

Answers
on page 126

KEEP SCORE ★ ❑ ❑ ❑ ❑ ❑ ❑ ❑ ❑ ❑ ❑ ❑ ❑ ❑ ❑ ❑ ❑ ❑ ❑

Merchants of Venice?

Well, there must be barbers at least, with all these poles

DAN KITWOOD/GETTY

17
changes

KEEP
SCORE

6min 25sec

Answers
on page 126

Double-Decker Fun

In Times Square, one photo doesn't quite square

1

2

3

4

5

6

0min 30sec

Answer
on page 126

What a Small World!

Oops! Sorry!! That song playing in your head now?

1

2

3

4

5

6

0min 45sec

Answer
on page 126

Stick Shift

Off we go, into the wild, blue yonder . . . or not

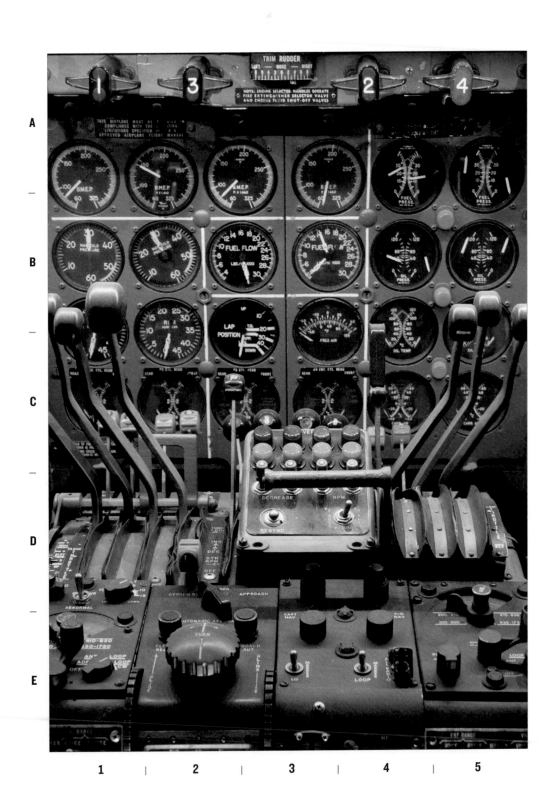

14
changes

KEEP
SCORE

❏
❏
❏
❏
❏
❏
❏
❏
❏
❏
❏
❏
❏
❏

⧗

4min 15sec

Answers
on page 126

Show Time

Bright lights, Big Macs

GEORGE ROSE/GETTY

22
changes

KEEP
SCORE

⏳
7min 15sec

Answers
on page 127

LIFE
CLASSICS

[
These puzzles were
specially created with
memorable photos
from the LIFE archives.
]

Port of Call: Margaritaville

Sure looks like it

ELIOT ELISOFON/LIFE

A
—
B
—
C
—
D
—
E

1 | 2 | 3 | 4 | 5

8
changes

KEEP
SCORE

❏ ❏
❏ ❏
❏ ❏
❏ ❏
❏

⧗
3min 15sec

Answers
on page 127

Lucky Fella

He's taking his shot on the wheel of fortune

A
—
B
—
C
—
D
—
E

1 | 2 | 3 | 4 | 5

10
changes

⧗
4 min 10 sec

Answers
on page 127

KEEP SCORE ★ ❏ ❏ ❏ ❏ ❏ ❏ ❏ ❏ ❏ ❏

Survivorwomen

Guests for lunch?

A
–
B
–
C
–
D
–
E

1 | 2 | 3 | 4 | 5

9
changes

KEEP
SCORE

❏
❏
❏
❏
❏
❏
❏
❏

⧗

2min 15sec

Answers
on page 127

T Minus 4 and Holding

It's time to get this rocket smokin'!

J. R. EYERMAN/LIFE

A

–

B

–

C

–

D

–

E

1   2   3   4   5

8
changes

⏳

3min 40sec

Answers
on page 127

KEEP SCORE ★ ❑ ❑ ❑ ❑ ❑ ❑ ❑ ❑

You're Sure He's Friendly?

Just make sure you count your fingers after finishing this one

NINA LEEN/LIFE

A

B

C

D

E

1   2   3   4   5

12
changes

⧗

4min 50sec

Answers
on page 127

KEEP SCORE ★ ❏ ❏ ❏ ❏ ❏ ❏ ❏ ❏ ❏ ❏ ❏ ❏

[ANSWERS]

Finished already? Let's see how you did.

[INTRODUCTION]

Page 3: Staring Contest
No. 1 (B1 to B2): This statue is getting a swollen head from all the attention. No. 2 (B2): It looks like someone's been doing repair work on the side. No. 3 (B3): He's flipping his (partial) head. No. 4 (B4): How does the song go, "He's got lemur eyes." No. 5 (C1): The wall is being extended. No. 6 (C3): He's so light, he floats. No. 7 (C5): Will the person who walked off with the Easter Island statue please put it back? No. 8 (D3): The itty-bitty stone has rolled away. No. 9 (E5): These tourists have gained a brand-new perspective.

[NOVICE]

Page 7: Remember to Floss No. 1 (A5 to B5): His big snout helps him sniff out tasty treats . . . like you. No. 2 (B4 to C4): Does anyone know if alligator teeth keep growing and growing? No. 3 (C1): Oh no, he used the pole as a toothpick again. No. 4 (C4): Good idea, face the giant carnivore! No. 5 (D1): His little toe is no more. No. 6 (D2): Purple makes a bold fashion statement. No. 7 (D4 to E5): Brushing helps keep the dentist away. No. 8 (E2 to E3): His dentist hopes he uses fluoridated toothpaste.

Page 8: Leap of Faith No. 1 (A3 to A5): The mountain slope has slipped away. Nos. 2 and 3 (C3): The bad plaid has caused a T-shirt temper tantrum. Watch it go purple from the bottom up. No. 4 (D2): The strap has flapped. No. 5 (D4 to D5): Would he still be grinning if he knew the cord had been cut? No. 6 (E2): Better not trust the rails around here. No. 7 (E3): He's footloose and fancy free. Or is it foot*less*?

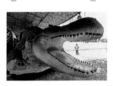

Page 10: Land of the Giants No. 1 (B1): Ah, more back support now. Nos. 2, 3, and 4 (B3): The blue tulip is missing its friend the green shoot, while the metal strap left the barrel to join the band. Nos. 5 and 6 (C3): One side of the tablecloth is stretching down while the other side has vanished. No. 7 (C4): The fence post is toast. No. 8 (C4 to D5): This little equine looks suspiciously familiar. No. 9 (D1): When did the horse move behind the chair?

Page 12: You've Heard of the Trojan Horse? No. 1 (A1): We could say, "the bolt has bolted," but we never, ever pun. No. 2 (A3 to A4): It seems it's just the force of its personality that keeps this elephant in the air. No. 3 (B2): The shirt logo is kaput. No. 4 (C2): The plywood has been cornered. No. 5 (C4): He's put his foot down. No. 6 (D2): Now the frame runs straight and true. Nos. 7 and 8 (D3): They've painted the panel red and added a side light. No. 9 (E1): The hydraulic foot must not

be needed anymore. We very much hope it's not needed.

Page 14: Stairway to Heaven No. 1 (A3): The tower is being bricked up. No. 2 (A5 to B5): Guess what, no antenna, no radio. Nos. 3 and 4 (B2): An extra blue balloon can't keep us from thinking one of these faces looks familiar. No. 5 (B3 to B4): It looks like the builders goofed on this section of the wall. Nos. 6 and 7 (E1): Don't trip on the missing step—or the longer gown.

Page 16: Tee Time
One of the golfers in photo No. 2 must be a vampire.

Page 17: Pass the Hot Sauce
The robot in photo No. 5 broke a tooth. That's what comes from chewing on metal.

Page 18: Crazy, Dude! No. 1 (A5): Shark's fin in the water, surfers take warning. No. 2 (B2 to B3): This doggie seems goggle-eyed over the local wildlife. Nos. 3 and 4 (C3): As one pooch licks his chops, another is losing his spots. No. 5 (C4): Ear missing in action. Nos. 6 and 7 (D3): Someone's putting his best foot forward as the board loses a star. No. 8 (D4): He looks like he's got a nose for trouble.

Page 20: Pumping Canine No. 1 (A5): Smoking may be permitted here. Or not. No. 2 (B2): This place takes changing light bulbs to new heights. No. 3 (C2): She's lost her credentials. No. 4 (D1 to E1): She must be wearing mood tights. No. 5 (D2 to E2): Her pants leg is just a little long. No. 6 (E5): Trust us, no one will notice the missing stripe.

Page 22: Circle of Friends No. 1 (A4): Their safety cable is gone. Nos. 2 and 3 (B4): She's got her arm out while he's put on his ridiculous hat. He always jumps with it. No. 4 (B5): Somehow he slipped his shoe on during freefall. No. 5 (C3): Bet you didn't know that altimeters can make funny faces? No. 6 (D3): He's sticking his tongue out at the altimeter. No. 7 (D4 to E4): The backpack inclines toward purple. No. 8 (D5): The clip has gone green.

Page 24: Head Over Heels No. 1 (A1): Exit foot, stage right, or house left, that is . . . never mind. No. 2 (A5 to B5): He's got both his arms out now. No. 3 (C2): She's misplaced her belly button. No. 4 (C3): Her shirt has fallen upwards. No. 5 (D4): A logo has washed off the shirt. No. 6 (E1): Her foot has rotated all the way around. No. 7 (E2): Her sleeve is feeling a bit bluish.

Page 25: Bumper-to-Bumper Traffic No. 1 (A2): A new car is making its way *up* the twisty road. Crash, boom, bang! Can't the driver read the traffic signs? No. 2 (A2 to B3): The new elastic SUVs can stretch on demand. No. 3 (C3): Now they can lock the doors of their vehicle. No. 4 (C4): The yellow side light has been replaced with an orange one. No. 5 (D3 to D4): The hedge has been trimmed from the bottom up. No. 6 (D5): It's hard to get a handle on what's missing from this car.

Page 26: Symmetry in Stone No. 1 (B3): Over time the minaret has just faded away. Nos. 2 and 3 (B4): After the tree reached for the sky, the arch reversed itself. No. 4 (B5): The balcony has been taken down for maintenance. No. 5 (C2): These three men look like brothers. No. 6 (C3): Reflections come and go in the reflecting pool. No. 7 (D5): A twin is catching up to her sister. No. 8 (E2 to E3): It wouldn't be a LIFE Picture Puzzle book without our rubber duckie!

Page 28: Please Don't Feed the Dino No. 1 (B4): Her cap is a blank slate, or at least blank fabric. No. 2 (B5): In a common but useful picture puzzle trick, the lad has popped a button. Nos. 3 and 4 (C2): The dino has added a spot to his head while his eyes are now a shade of green. Let's hope those aren't signs of hunger. No. 5 (C3): She's added two buttons to her top. That's the last button change you will see in this book. (Liar, liar, pants on fire.) No. 6 (D1 to D2): His teeth are growing. Now we know he's hungry. No. 7 (D3 to D4): She's got diamonds on the front of her skirt. (Sing along if you know the words.) No. 8 (E3 to E4): The hem has been let down. No. 9 (E5): His shorts are suffering from droopy pant leg syndrome.

Page 30: Space Age Dubai No. 1 (A2 to B3): It's a known fact: Skyscrapers melt in the desert sun. No. 2 (C2): Count them, the parasol has three ferrules on top. No. 3 (C4 to C5): The building has lost a band. No. 4 (D2): How does the canopy stay up without its pole? Heat waves. Nos. 5 and 6 (D3): She's shed her earring and her blouse is leafing out. No. 7 (D4): Blue seems to be the color of choice for parasols. Nos. 8 and 9 (E1): An arch next door has disappeared as the parapet wall has merged together. No. 10 (E5): A shadow has fled the noonday sun.

Page 32: Flag Day No. 1 (A1 to C5): It's a rare blue-sky day on the moon. No. 2 (A5): A full moon shines down on the astronauts. Hey, wait a minute! No. 3 (B4 to C4): The lighter lunar gravity has lengthened the flag. (Okay, that makes no sense but we were hoping you wouldn't notice.) No. 4 (C1): If that's the lunar lander, then what's casting the shadow below? No. 5 (C2): We think the blue stripe looks just as nice as the red ones. No. 6 (D3): Although the flag's shadow should be longer now, somehow it's shorter. No. 7 (E2): Put that rock back where you found it. No. 8 (E3 to E4): If an astronaut's shadow reverses itself on the moon, will anyone hear it?

Page 34: What's Buggin' You? No. 1 (A4 to A5): Not only is it a giant flower, it's a giant blue flower. No. 2 (B4): The tree has grown an extra strange fruit. Nos. 3, 4, and 5 (C1): It can be hard to read a moving sign, but the exit sign is not as backwards as it used to be. On the other hand, don't these windows seem taller in the daylight? No. 6 (D3): A stealth antenna doesn't cast a shadow. No. 7 (D5): Another diner has been seated. No. 8 (E1 to E2): The bug steps forward bravely in the garden. Screams of restaurant patrons can be heard in the background.

Page 36: Fishy Business

4	1
2	3

Page 37: Everything's Coming Up Roses

4	2
1	3

Page 38: Balancing Act No. 1 (A2): The green pole has popped up. No. 2 (A3 to C3): A good unicyclist can balance facing left or right. No. 3 (A3): But how did he manage that trick with his hand? No. 4 (B5): They're cutting back the trees in the park. No. 5 (C1): A hole underneath the slide has been filled in. No. 6 (C2 to E2): Even though the pole is yellow now, that doesn't mean it's chicken. It's a pole. No. 7 (D1): Some thieves stole play equipment last night. No. 8 (D3 to E3): With cyclists riding on top, they decided to provide the bridge with extra support. No. 9 (E3): But they've moved the green pole further back. No. 10 (E5): The slide loves listening to the song "I Melt With You."

Page 40: Nice Kitties, Nice Kitties
No. 1 (A3): Everything grows rapidly in tropical climates. No. 2 (B1 to B2): Don't shoot until you see the blue of his eye. No. 3 (B4): Two whiskers have become one. No. 4 (B5): The ox has traded in its blanket for a blue one. No. 5 (C2): Did the tiger really need a longer, sharper tooth? Nos. 6 and 7 (C4): This tiger has lost a tooth. Perhaps that's why the two boys are cautiously paying a visit. No. 8 (C5): The grazing doe is winking about something. No. 9 (E4): Keep quiet about the extra toe. The tiger's quite sensitive about it.

[MASTER]

Page 43: And the Winner Is . . . No. 1 (A1): You decide: Extra cameras—neighborhood watch or Big Brother? No. 2 (A2): Two bricks had an urge to merge. No. 3 (A3): Her hat grows greener in the sunlight. No. 4 (A5): Don't flip out over the walkway sign. No. 5 (B2 to C2): It seems like a nose band bit the dust. No. 6 (C1 to C2): The wall decor is being simplified. Nos. 7 and 8 (C5): Careless, careless. Someone misspelled the town of Zirc and used the wrong color on its coat of arms. No. 9 (D2): This little horsey has a big hoof. No. 10 (D4): And this little horsey's leg is a tad short.

Page 44: Cliffhanger No. 1 (A3): And today's climb will be just a little more challenging courtesy of the famous flexible cliff. No. 2 (A3 to C3): Let's hope his backup rope is well secured. No. 3 (B5): Even climbing bags get the blues in the mountain cold. No. 4 (C5): The satchel's handle has acquired a new logo. No. 5 (D1): A cliff looms taller in the distance. No. 6 (D3): Do bigger feet help in climbing? No. 7 (D5): Logos: Easy come, easy go. Nos. 8 and 9 (E2): As the strap handles proliferate, the glacier slides over a drumlin. No. 10 (E4 to E5): The rope's shadow has been severed.

Page 46: A Walk on the Wild Side No. 1 (A3): Two shuttles in orbit at once? Nah, couldn't be. No. 2 (A3 to A4): A flange has taken up orbit all on its own. Nos. 3 and 4 (B1): In space no one can hear a 3 become an 8. Or new vent holes pop open. No. 5 (B2): Red, blue, they're all just stripes. No. 6 (C5): Two handle bars have been retrofitted as one. No. 7 (D3): Yes, yes, it's another big boot. There's an epidemic of them this year. No. 8 (D5): This must be the ninth astronaut. No. 9 (E5): And he's an astronaut without a country, or at least a flag.

Page 48: Hey There, Little Fella No. 1 (A3): My, this tree is limber. Nos. 2 and 3 (B4): Did his big ear help him hear the tree trunk disappear? No. 4 (B5): Her hair is more there. No. 5 (C2 to D2): His handler is playing peekaboo. No. 6 (C3): A bridle flashes blue. No. 7 (C4): The little guy's been given free rein. No. 8 (C5): The pink strip is being swept away. No. 9 (D1): The hoof is getting hoofier. No. 10 (D5): Now that's a horse's tail.

Page 50: Celestial Season Nos. 1 and 2 (A2): As the sarsen stone on the left gets a little taller, the nearby capstone grows a touch longer. No. 3 (A3): These capstones have joined forces. No. 4 (B4): Wait a minute! Has the heel stone vanished? Nos. 5 and 6 (B5): The cloth band has been redyed and, apparently, this isn't Stonehenge any more. Nos. 7, 8, and 9 (C3): The flower pot has moved to the left, lost its legs, and witnessed a yellow flower go pink. No. 10 (D2): She knows that a picture lasts longer. No. 11 (E4 to E5): He'd better check the ground for his missing viewfinder.

Page 52: Imperial Waters No. 1 (A4): The cupola has gently sagged down. Darn that modern prefab construction. No. 2 (B3): A green diamond has invaded the yellow ones. No. 3 (B5): The crowning ball is now quite small. No. 4 (C3 to D3): These windows have bridged the gap between. No. 5 (C5 to D5): Workers are busy extending the second floor. No. 6 (D1): He's wearing chameleon trunks. No. 7 (D2 to D3): While they were at it, the construction crew also lowered this ledge. No. 8 (D3): He's diving for pennies. Times are tough. No. 9 (D4): Very funny. Now put the sign back. No. 10 (E1): Doesn't he realize that three's a crowd. No. 11 (E4): He's slowly drifting across the pool. No. 12 (E5): The stairs are a bit grander now.

Page 54: A Slippery Slope No. 1 (A1): The new window really lets the light in. No. 2 (A3): Who keeps bricking up the walls. No. 3 (B1): Wink, wink. No. 4 (B3): Now there's more room for poster proclamations. No. 5 (C1): The barrier's been lifted. No. 6 (C3): She's got a new pretty pink hat. No. 7 (C4): His hat is getting a bit mossy. No. 8 (D1 to E1): This boy must be sliding backwards. No. 9 (D3 to D4): The icy patch is twice as slippery (and twice as big) now.

Page 56: Poetry in Motion No. 1 (A2 to B3): Lowering his arm gives him more lift on the way down. We think. No. 2 (A3): Heads up. Or head up. Whatever. No. 3 (A5 to B5): These windows make us shutter. Okay, we do use puns. Really bad ones. No. 4 (C2): The extra canopy has a secret antigravity device keeping it up. No. 5 (C3 to D4): They must be rowing backwards. No. 6 (C5): The deck looks better in brown. No. 7 (E1 to E2): Standing in boats is a good way to swamp them. No. 8 (E3): The kayak has had a quick paint job. No. 9 (E4): Santa's left the river. No. 10 (E4 to E5): But, hey, we've gained a new kayak.

Page 58: Don't Get Snookered His hand is empty in photo No. 3.

Page 59: **It's Alive!**
Photo No. 5 points the way to a free lunch.

Page 60: **Sittin' on Top of the World**
No. 1 (A2): The top triangle has blown away.
No. 2 (B2): Buddha is in his shrine and all is well with the world. No. 3 (B3): Shades make the man. No. 4 (B3 to B4): Did you know that knit caps expand in low air pressure? Either that, or his skull is swelling up. No. 5 (C3 to C4): The mountain logo has been upended. No. 6 (C5 to D5): It's true. The Himalayas are still growing. No. 7 (D2): The cord and the shrine are parting ways. No. 8 (D4): Please don't use this carabiner. No. 9 (E2): The sign is not as wordy as it used to be. No. 10 (E3): Big knee pads make kneeling easier.

Page 62: **Triangulation** No. 1 (A3 to B4): It's a very pointy pyramid, isn't it? No. 2 (D1): The hot sun has bleached his T-shirt totally white. No. 3 (D2): Today is not a big hair day. No. 4 (D4 to D5): Try saying "blue" when it's yellow. Come on, try it. No. 5 (D5): The wheel well is no more.
Nos. 6 and 7 (E3): She must be double-jointed and he's misplaced his shadow. No. 8 (E3 to E4): And her shadow has a new slant on things. No. 9 (E4): While the girl in question is suddenly feeling modest.

Page 64: **On Safari** No. 1 (A3): It's a rail with lofty ambitions. No. 2 (A5): Her splotches have blotched. No. 3 (C1 to D2): Safety vests don't have to be orange, do they? No. 4 (C2 to C3): His sleeve has rolled down. No. 5 (C4): Two boards got bored with being single. No. 6 (D3): For want of a bolt, a trailer was lost. Better replace it. No. 7 (D5): Two lights are better than one. No. 8 (E1): A strap has been bisected. No. 9 (E3): No light is definitely worse than one. No. 10 (E5): The word *turning* keeps turning. Well, really it's a mirror image but we like repeating *turning*.

Page 66: **One Hump or Two?** No. 1 (B1): The camel nods yes. No. 2 (B3): Tower Bridge is fading in the fog. No. 3 (B4): His shirt has lost its global status. No. 4 (C3): The lamp is so light, it floats in the air. No. 5 (C4): Somewhere, there's a yellow pom-pom nestled on the grass. No. 6 (C4 to D4): The man in the suit has joined the CPP, or the Camel Protection Program. But he's not a camel. We're confused. Nos. 7 and 8 (D2): As the leg gets shorter, the blanket gets longer. No. 9 (D4): This leg just gets longer.

Page 68: **Batter Up!** No. 1 (A1): One prayer flag seems to be swelling up. No. 2 (A3): Another flag has fluttered away. Nos. 3 and 4 (C2): Not only is the batter edging closer to the pitcher, he's also getting bigger. No. 5 (C3): Who's that in the outfield? No. 6 (C4): It seems that altitude sickness causes pitch-

ers to throw the ball in the wrong direction. Nos. 7 and 8 (C5): Now why did the tent turn orange and where did that second batter come from? No. 9 (D2 to E2): Zipperless tents are the latest rage. No. 10 (D3): No one will notice one more rock on the playing field.

Page 70: **If a Tree Falls . . .** No. 1 (C2): The missing sign was probably used for firewood. Nos. 2 and 3 (C3): As a teenage girl clambered onto the downed tree, the tunnel began to shrink. No. 4 (D1): Her jacket has gone from hot to cool. No. 5 (D2): A rock is taking a rest at the edge of the road. No. 6 (D3): Doesn't that boy know there's a camper heading toward him? No. 7 (D5): The front of the station wagon has been chopped off. Nos. 8 and 9 (E4): The license plate thief has been busy while Mr. Bad Directions has been playing with this sign.

Page 72: **The Flowers that Bloom in the Spring**

6	3
5	4
2	1

Page 73: **Sky High**

4	5
2	3
6	1

Page 74: **Pucker Up**
In photo No. 6 a palm tree doesn't grow at this festival.

Page 75: **Big Birds**
His pants are minus a stripe in photo No. 2.

Page 76: **In the Village** No. 1 (A2): The headlands are heading out to sea. No. 2 (A3): The lighthouse has been built up. No. 3 (A4 to B4): To handle all the crowds, the government is lengthening the building. No. 4 (B3 to B4): The lobster boat looks to be ahead of schedule. No. 5 (C2 to D2): The pole has vaulted away. No. 6 (C3 to D3): Look away for a moment and a chimney disappears. No. 7 (D2): As part of the green movement, the church is relying more on natural light. No. 8 (D3): The barn door is also going green. No. 9 (E2): The house has gained a win-

dow. No. 10 (E3): And lost a chair. No. 11 (E4): Please don't fence off the street. No. 12 (E5): Window installation has hit this town in a big way.

[EXPERT]

Page 79: Candyland

3	8	1
9	5	7
6	2	4

Page 80: Fair Weather Ferry No. 1 (A2): A skyscraper has flipped its top. Nos. 2 and 3 (B1): The building has racked up more floors but lost its corporate sponsorship. No. 4 (B3): Instead of a lady, the building vanishes—at least partly. No. 5 (B5 to C5): This place has more window offices now. No. 6 (C1): Really wide windows usually mean executive suites. No. 7 (C2): This little dormer climbs up the roof. No. 8 (C3 to D3): While this little dormer falls off. No. 9 (D3): The red speedboat seems a little seasick. No. 10 (D4): The palm has been replanted behind the RV. No. 11 (E2): A boat motored away. No. 12 (E5): And a buoy bobs.

Page 82: Like a Neon Cowboy No. 1 (A2 to A3): Anybody got a match? No. 2 (A3): With a thumb like this, he must be good at hitchhiking. No. 3 (B1 to C1): More lights mean brighter nights. No. 4 (B4): With this camera, LVPD really sees all. No. 5 (C3): His spur's done gone. No. 6 (C5): This boot was made for kicking. No. 7 (D2): The hyphen pivots. Nos. 8 and 9 (D3): The store has sold all but one of its gifts and someone flipped an *S*. No. 10 (D4): Who tore the poster down? No. 11 (E2): He's 78 now. He looks good for his age. No. 12 (E4): Don't try to sit on this stool. What stool? Exactly. No. 13 (E5): Are you experienced?

Page 84: A San Francisco Treat No. 1 (A4): The two tall stacks are on top of it all, or at least on top of the street. No. 2 (B3): Let's hope the missing vent isn't really necessary. No. 3 (C3): The new windows are low-riders. No. 4 (C4): Someone shut the window. Nos. 5 and 6 (D1): One vehicle sports three headlights and the orange car is moving up fast. No. 7 (D2): Once again, it's so easy to spin a "6" into a "9." No. 8 (D4 to E4): The Powell and Market sign tries to center itself. No. 9 (D4): Number 4 is no more. No. 10 (D5): The hydrant has a twin. No. 11 (E1): The road repair crew has repaired the repair. No. 12 (E2): The cable car's plow is whole, we mean it has no hole. No. 13 (E3): A manhole cover has been covered.

Page 86: Pass the Mustard Nos. 1 and 2 (A2): The antenna goes down as the piling goes up. No. 3 (B1): Don't frown but there's an extra skiff in town. No. 4 (B4 to B5): A cabin cruiser cruises home. No. 5 (C4): He's eating a mega-dog. Nos. 6 and 7 (D2): Can you handle it? The bag's handle will no longer

serve, while the pot's handle hides behind Mom's leg. No. 8 (D3): Does she realize that she's got a dog in the pot and on the bun? No. 9 (D5): Even if he notices that it's missing, chances are that he'll never find his watch in all that sand. No. 10 (E1): A cantaloupe has joined the picnic. No. 11 (E2 to E3): The reflection is a reflection of itself. No. 12 (E3): Redundancy in planning: There are four people and five cups. No. 13 (E4): His pant leg dangles down. No. 14 (E5): He's digging his foot out of the sand.

Page 88: Pomp and Circumstance One of the wheels in photo No. 5 must be in the shop for repair.

Page 89: In the House of the Mouse Mickey must be rolling his eyes in photo No. 4.

Page 90: Clown Town No. 1 (A2): Neuhaus is new now. Or at least, its signage is new. Get it? No. 2 (A5): Turn right, no, turn left. No. 3 (B2): If green thumbs signify good gardeners, what do green noses indicate? Don't answer that. Nos. 4 and 5 (B3): A new stranger in the crowd seems to disapprove of the clown with vulcan ears. No. 6 (B4): A jacket stud has flip-flopped. Nos. 7 and 8 (C3): The clowns broke their chains and grabbed a poster to celebrate their freedom. No. 9 (C4): His glockenspiel jacket now goes one note lower. Plink, plink, plonk. No. 10 (C5 to D5): Her, um, er, his stockings are a lovely shade of green now. No. 11 (C5): Ouch! A sneaker's been surgically removed. No. 12 (D5): My, what a big foot you have! Is it better to stomp with? No. 13 (E2): These cuffs are very yellow—and very tall. No. 14 (E3 to E4): The post has been repositioned and significantly elongated. *E-l-o-n-g-a-t-e-d*, now isn't that just an elongated way of saying lengthened? Hmmmm, nine letters, ten letters, never mind.

Page 92: Mirror, Mirror on the Wall No. 1 (A1): Now there's a reflector behind the reflections. No. 2 (A2): The light in the mirror is no more. No. 3 (B1 to C1): The stripes on his shirt are a lovely shade of mustard now. By the way, we're lying about the lovely. No. 4 (B2): Either the beret is getting bigger or his head has been shrunk. No. 5 (B3 to C4): The reflection in this mirror is a mirror-mirror image. It's like a double-negative in English. Or not. No. 6 (B4 to C4): The man in the mirror is getting closer and closer. Nos. 7 and 8 (B4): One of these mirrors has borrowed the reflection of the man previously mentioned to replace the reflection of the frame of the other mirror. Do you find all these mirrors as confusing as we do? No. 9 (B5): The jet has flown past the frame. But where are all those little people going to stay? No. 10 (C2): Longer horns produce louder notes. No. 11 (C4): Someone's ducked out of the reflection. No. 12 (D2): His footstep casts no shadow. No. 13 (E3 to E4): The heat of the Grecian sun is softening the brass.

[GENIUS]

Page 95: Hangin' Out No. 1 (A1 to B1): Without flowers, you don't need a vase. No. 2 (A2 to B2): Elastic paintings can be s-t-r-e-t-c-h-e-d to fit. No. 3 (A3): His new wool cap fits perfectly. No. 4 (A5): Who's to say which way is up. No. 5 (B2): Clearly, fame has gone to his head. No. 6 (B3): He must be practicing sign language. No. 7 (C1): The cherub is cavorting. No. 8 (C2): Does *Dad Peace* mean no yelling? Probably not. No. 9 (C5): He doesn't look it, but he should be more comfortable without a tie. No. 10 (D1): She's got a fan, a big fan. No. 11 (D3): The storm tossed the ship to and fro. No. 12 (E2): Wild animal alert! The wood trim has become beaver fodder. No. 13 (E4): This painting is so weighty, it's sagged to the floor. No. 14 (E5): Long aprons appear to be "in" this year.

Page 96: Changing of the Guard (Again) Nos. 1 and 2 (A1): Part of the roof has drooped over the edge and a lotus blossom tile has fallen off. Nos. 3 and 4 (A3 to B3): Graffiti artists have been messing with the logograms. No. 5 (A4): Someone's stuck up an extra tile here. No. 6 (C1): Two bricks, two bricks, two bricks are one. No. 7 (C2): If you're going to wear a yellow hat, it might as well be tall. No. 8 (C3): The top of his helmet has visibility fatigue. No. 9 (C5): He's quite a tall gent. Nos. 10 and 11 (D2): This horn won't blow and his beard looks fake. No. 12 (D3): Here's a tip, the rod has lost its . . . tip. No. 13 (D4): On the other hand, Gabriel can really make *this* horn blow. The guy is named Gabriel. Don't ask us how we know. We know. No. 14 (D5): His costume billows in the breeze. No. 15 (E1): He's so light, he doesn't need feet. No. 16 (E4): It's a mega-ribbon.

Page 98: Let Me Out! Nos. 1, 2, and 3 (A3): There are more stars on the longer field of blue but one has slipped off, and the shuttle's tail rises high to the, well, not sky. No. 4 (A4 to B4): The satellite has tacked on an extension. No. 5 (A5): An astronaut floats freely near the . . . roof. It just doesn't have the same ring to it. No. 6 (B3): American flags don't sag, they just get longer. No. 7 (C2): Better not try a wheelie now. No. 8 (C3): They're shy one porthole. That's what it's called, right? No. 9 (C4): The display case has quite a hangover, I mean overhang. No. 10 (D2): Has anyone seen a darlin' little *c*? No. 11 (D3): Without its foot, an *L* is just an *I*. Oh my. No. 12 (E1): The spot is bare of chair. No. 13 (E2): He's shambling toward the right. No. 14 (E3): Mission Control, we have liftoff. No. 15 (E4): This kid comes from the Land of Mirrors.

Page 100: The Curiosity Shoppe No. 1 (A2): He knows when to keep his mouth shut. Nos. 2 and 3 (A3): Will Mr. Nosy notice the needlessly missing horn on the opposite wall? No. 4 (A4): These wooden skis are the extra-large model with jumbo splinters. No. 5 (B1): The person who buys this uniform better know how to sew. No. 6 (B2): Swap a *P* for a *B* and you have a whole different kind of mushroom. No. 7 (B3): A customer must have bought the blue letter *A*. No. 8 (B4): The wooden soldier is suffering from some shrinkage. No. 9 (C2 to D2): These days the good old Union Jack is feeling a little blue. No. 10 (C5 to D5): Yellow is the new red, at least for

hats. No. 11 (D1): My, grandmother. What a big putter you have. Nos. 12 and 13 (D2): From the look of these two signs, English may not be this storekeeper's forte. No. 14 (D3): The floor has been stripe-swiped. No. 15 (E1): The shaft has a bigger grip now. And we don't mean anything by that. No. 16 (D5 to E5): The hat looks even more ridiculous now.

Page 102: Merchants of Venice? No. 1 (B4 to C4): The sun wheel spins. All is well with the universe. No. 2 (B5): Guess who joined the Chimney Relocation Program? Nos. 3 and 4 (C1): We're two flags up and one chimney down. Nos. 5 and 6 (C2): With one building losing a window, the cathedral decrees "Let the light in." No. 7 (C3): No matter how you spell it, Venice always starts with a *V*, doesn't it? No. 8 (C3 to D3): He's surrounded by horns. No. 9 (C4): The stacks look overstacked. No. 10 (D1): Every now and then you have to be daring and try a different-colored spiral. No. 11 (D2): The red poles are reaching for the sky. No. 12 (E1): This powerboat is going incognito—and numberless. No. 13 (E1 to E2): There's more oar than before. No. 14 (E2): The rumors about the pole's translucentness are baseless. Or is it the pole that is baseless? No. 15 (E3 to E4): Swell, the boat's hit a swell. No. 16 (E3): And it's lost its reflection. No. 17 (E4): Do they have one more lion to roar or one more mouth to feed?

Page 104: Double-Decker Fun The big blue LG sign in Photo No. 1 is one dot down. Yes, yes, it's a very small change but this is the Genius section, isn't it? (Is it? Better check. Okay, yes it is.) So deal with it.

Page 105: What a Small World! The lad has pulled in his arm in photo No. 6. Check it out, it's really there . . . or not there. You know what we mean. But do we?

Page 106: Stick Shift No. 1 (A2 to A4): The numbers are button-swapping. No. 2 (A3): The words on the trim gauge are getting into a similar game. No. 3 (B1): This knob only looks more important than the rest. Nos. 4 and 5 (B2): The arrow hand is supposed to turn, not the whole dial! How nice, a lap counter. There must be a pool in the back of the plane—where the engine's supposed to be. No. 6 (B3): For want of a screw, a cockpit was lost. No. 7 (C5): Does anyone know what this extra light is for? No. 8 (C5 to D5): Let's hope we won't need the missing lever later. Otherwise, we just got shafted. Nos. 9 and 10 (D1): A taller toggle isn't necessarily abnormal, but someone labelled it that way. No. 11 (D3): The approach label is approaching the middle. No. 12 (D4): Someone flipped the switch but not the shadow. No. 13 (E4): There's a brand-new switch to fiddle with. No. 14 (E5): The dial has lost its stripe.

Page 108: Show Time No. 1 (A1): These days, one window less looks out on old Broadway. Nos. 2 and 3 (A1 to B1): Don't fear the power of the green arm or you, too, will face an impossible date! No. 4 (A1): Copy's been busy rewriting the subhead. No. 5 (A2): The *N* is feeling a bit backward today. No. 6 (A2 to B3): Sure thing, the sign's been redesigned. No. 7 (A3): Click! Lights on in the office. No. 8 (A4 to B4): Click! Lights off in this one. No. 9 (A5): Someone's got a nice big office with a picture window now. No. 10 (B2 to C2): You've got to be kidding! They really can't spell PALACE? No. 11 (B2): It's a funny-looking *E*. No. 12 (B5): It's amazing that they got rid of even one light. Of course, one can't tell the difference, can one? No. 13 (C1): The mask is blind to all the glitter and glamour. No. 14 (C3): The streetlight is a twin. No. 15 (C4 to C5): The golden arches hang down in the middle. No. 16 (D2 to D3): It's a scavenger hunt. Next we find a missing THE. Nos. 17, 18, and 19 (D3): The lamp pole has used vanishing cream from *The Body Shop*, Times Square Information has lost its center, and the *i* is head over heels. No. 20 (D3 to E3): The excess vanishing cream has dripped down on the wheel. No. 21 (D5): The taxi ad must be designed to be read in a rearview mirror—but it's on the side of the car. No. 22 (E5): You didn't hear it from us, but big bumpers come in handy with New York City drivers.

[LIFE CLASSICS]

Page 111: Port of Call: Margaritaville
No. 1 (A1 to B2): Without wind, more sail won't help. No. 2 (B2 to C2): Who turned on the Klingon cloaking shield? Shut it down before the mast disappears altogether. No. 3 (C1): One of the mooring lines slipped off. No. 4 (C5): Another boat has dropped anchor. No. 5 (D2): The hyphen is migrating up. No. 6 (E2): A dangling rope dangles lower. No. 7 (E2 to E3): The pile has rotted away. No. 8 (E3): It looks like the shadow repair crew has been at work here.

Page 112: Lucky Fella No. 1 (A2): It's dangerous to jump off when the ferris wheel is in motion but it seems he did it anyway. No. 2 (A3): In a blink of an eye, a sister became a stranger. No. 3 (A4 to A5): The bolt's been sheared away. No. 4 (B1 to B2): An extra crossbar has been added. No. 5 (B3 to C3): The end of the footrest has been capped. No. 6 (B5): It's a bigger spaceship now. No. 7 (C1): Naw, that was a spare girder. No. 8 (C3 to D3): Was that the sound of a snapping cable? No. 9 (D1 to E1): Curfew rules: No one leaves this trailer until we draw the door back in. No one. Got that? No. 10 (D4): For fairs that move around every week, it helps to have everything clearly labelled and numbered.

Page 114: Survivorwomen No. 1 (B1): We cannot tell a lie. We photochopped down this cherry tree. Except it wasn't cherry. Nos. 2 and 3 (B3): A bear asks the silent question, "Got milk?" and a camper is blissfully unaware that her pan can't be handled. No. 4 (B5): The boulder has a bigger shoulder. No. 5 (C2): The new thermos keeps a lot more cool. No. 6 (C3): Did the bear get the milk? No. 7 (C3 to C4): Her sleeve has slipped. No. 8 (D1): The plate has been unclipped. No. 9 (D5): The can slides into view.

Page 116: T Minus 4 and Holding No. 1 (B2): Watch out, the rocket's been untethered. Blast-off imminent! Nos. 2 and 3 (C2): Gain a stripe and lose a lamp. It's about even-steven. No. 4 (D2): I've been through the desert on a rocket with no number. No, that's not quite right. Back to square one. No. 5 (D3 to D4): On smoking, everything goes kaboom! No. 6 (E1): It's a big, old garbage barrel, and even bigger now. No. 7 (E2): The fuel truck has shed its chains. No. 8 (E5): Don't worry, that's just a left-over leg from the last test flight.

Page 118: You're Sure He's Friendly? Nos. 1 and 2 (A2): He's got a big collar and really, really big hair. No. 3 (A2 to A3): The cable's down again … but this one doesn't have anything to do with the Internet. No. 4 (A3 to B3): Bet he's really proud of his horns. No. 5 (B3 to C3): A nose like this is meant for sniffing. No. 6 (C1): He's tucked his shirt in. No. 7 (C2): Another darn rope snapped. No. 8 (C5): On hot days, palm trees pull up their trunks inside their fronds. If you believe that, we've got a bridge in Brooklyn that's for sale. No. 9 (D1 to E1): How hot is it? It's so hot, the sun is burning away the shadows. No. 10 (D5): Hope you didn't have anything at stake at these coordinates. Get it? Har, har! No. 11 (E2): Lately, many giraffes are flocking to Hollywood plastic surgeons to get their hooves uncloven. No. 12 (D4 to E4): His leg strap has been unwrapped.

Synchronized Walking

You know what they say, "The bigger they are, the harder they fall."

JUST ONE MORE

CARSTEN KOALL/GETTY

14 changes

KEEP SCORE

4min 25sec

Solve this and become a true puppet, I mean, puzzle master.

ANSWERS No. 1 (A1 to B1): The tackle's been snipped. **No. 2** (A4): A flag flaps freely in the breeze. **No. 3** (A5): It's true, Alice. There are growth hormones for statues. **No. 4** (B2): The tackle is still there but, say goodbye to the block. **No. 5** (B3): The statue lifted up her skirts and sashayed away. **No. 6** (C1): The lamp has fading lamp disease. **No. 7** (C3): A window descends. **No. 8** (C5): Let the arrows (or are they wings?) point the way. **No. 9** (D1): He must be a member of the Hair Club for Men. **No. 10** (E1): Don't shake hands with this fellow. **No. 11** (E2): She's got no sole. **Nos. 12 and 13** (E4): Water has nowhere to drain and the stripe has split asunder. **No. 14** (E5): This guy's popped a button.

A — B — C — D — E

1   2   3   4   5